Married

Celibate

And Saved

A test of Love, Patience, and Faith

ISBN: 978-0-615-24641-3

ACKNOWLEDGEMENT

First, I would like to thank God and my Lord and Savior Jesus Christ, for seeing me through some of the most difficult times in my life. In addition, I would like to thank my family who has been there for us not only in spiritual needs, but also in physical needs. You have demonstrated a true workmanship during my time of need. And a special thanks to Mother Georgia Wallace and the late Deacon Lester Vickerson for being a spiritual guide. I love you all. May God bless you richly about all that you could ask or think in Jesus name.

DEDICATION

This book is dedicated to my beloved late husband Mr. Gary Lee Hill, for without him this book would not exists. May he rest in peace.

TABLE OF CONTENTS

1 Growing Up……………………………………………..1

2 How We met…………………………………………..…5

3 Married …………………………………..……………..15

4 Celibate …………………………..…………….………23

5 Fighting Temptations…………………………………26

6 And Saved…………………………………………..…30

7 When Loved One Leaves …………………………...45

8 "When It Rains, It Pours"…………………………..…62

9 I Just Wanted to Get Out ……………………...…..…76

Moving On………………………………....………81

Final Thought…………………………………..……83

Scriptures for Reading………………………….…84

Sexless Marriages …………………………....………85

1

Growing Up

I was a young girl living at home with my mother, step-dad, grandmother, grandfather, my two sisters and brother. Also, My Aunt Tina, who kept trouble going all the time, her boyfriend, and our cousins. People were always moving in and moving out of our house. Some were family and others were renters. One thing for sure, growing up with the Johnson's, there was never a dull moment.

And they were the funniest people I had ever seen. They loved mimicking and cracking jokes about other folks, especially my grandma Rosette and Aunt Jean. They should have been comedians. But my Grandma's main target was my granddad, who we called, Jay Bird. However, he did not see anything funny when she picked at him; he only got irritated with her. I never understood why she enjoyed aggravating him so much, until I asked her how did she get a scar on her arm? Gosh! She went back to 1940, when she was in a fight with a woman who was flirting with my granddad and she demonstrated the whole fight.

Nevertheless, my Grandma was a faithful churchgoer. I did not grow up in church, but my sisters and I always went to church with our Grandma on Easter Sundays and Homecoming, which was the first Sunday in August or Easter Sunday at Mount Sani Baptist Church in Gay, Georgia. Back then, I enjoyed the long rides. We would see horses chewing on the green grass, cows resting on the big ball of hay, chickens running in the field, and a waterfall. Eggs' hunting was the best part of going church. I would run around in the field trying to find as many eggs as I could. Some adults helped us find eggs. Oh boy, that was so much fun. Don't get me wrong, church service was good and long. If you were not saved, the beat of the drums made you want to be saved. It was a Baptist church, you know how they do. I remember the song I would hear every first Sunday. *"When the storm of life comes raging, Lord, stand by me."* That was that soul shaking music.

However, as time went on, a new generation was being born. My older sister Gwen had her first child Mekasha and then her second child two years later. She met and married Toisy; they added three more additions to her family. Then, my younger sister, Poot, had her first child, Nathan. She was another troublemaker, but she was funnier with hers. She could not get along with hardly anyone in the house or neighborhood and she ran away every boarder from the house. Then I got pregnant. And for the next four years, someone in our house was pregnant. I was trying to hide mine, knowing that, *"What is done in the dark will come to the light."* Boy isn't that the truth. One evening, my grandma and brother were sitting in the living room and I was on the front porch sitting on my bike thinking about what I was going to do. Then all of a sudden, I fell off. I was trying to get up before anyone saw me lying on the porch. However, my brother heard me fall and he ran straight to the door. When he saw me lying on the porch, he said out loud, "Lisa fell. 'She pregnant ain't she?" Then I heard Grandma say, "I don't know." So one day my grandma decided to put her sister, Aunt Jean to investigate. Aunt Jean was bold. She came into my room, while Grandma was listening outside the door, and asked me if I was pregnant. However, before I could answer her, she told me to lie down on the bed.

After I lay down, she put her two fingers under my neck to see if she could feel two hearts beat (That was how they did it in those days). Then she said, "Yep, you're pregnant." And she walked out the room. A few minutes later, I heard her tell my grandmother, "Yeah Rosa, she's pregnant." I started panicking. There I was, the *"good girl'* who didn't get into any trouble, was about to disappoint my family by getting pregnant. Grandma spread the news than a roadrunner. It seemed like it shocked everybody. All my life, from my perspective, I was looked at as the *good girl*.

People didn't know how much pressure being the *good girl* had on me. Having a child disappointed some of my family because they had higher expectations for me, and others treated me as if they had never done anything wrong. I was heart broken by what I heard from the people who used to give me great compliments; their sweet words became bitter sweet. I had one mean, old, tobacco-chewing Great-Aunt who called us out our name. She would say that we would be nothing but hoes and she even called us the bitches. Those comments began to shape and mold me to become bitter, angry, grudge holding and a magnet for negative thinking, which later had an effect on my life.

Nevertheless, my main concern was my mom's reaction, because I did not want to disappoint her. She was the nicest person I have ever known and I loved very much. When the news had gotten to her, she did not say a word. And that was the first time I'd notice that my mom had never complained too much about negatives things, nor have I ever heard her harshly criticize us for our mistakes. But she had always encouraged us to set better goals for ourselves and strive for the best and get an education.

2

How We Met

Later that night, I went to bed thinking about what I was going to do. After I had fallen to sleep, I dreamed about a man wearing beige shorts. It was a vague glimpse of this man; therefore I could not clearly see his face. As the months went by, I had my son, Zay, in May, and my mom helped me out with the diapers, until I got a job. Later in May, my mom and step-dad moved out and got an apartment on Rock Street. My son and I were traveling back and forth between my mom's and grandma's house. But on this particular weekend, I was over my mom's house. She did not have a telephone so I went down stairs to use the phone in the rent office. And while I was on the phone, I heard a man behind me talking. However, I didn't look back because my focus was with the person on the phone. I didn't know that it was Gary trying to get my attention. After I finished my conversation, I hung up the phone and went back upstairs to my room.

Then a few days later, I was walking to the store and Gary stopped and asked, "Are you going to the store?" I said, "Yeah." Then he pulled out a twenty-dollar bill and asked me to bring him back a bag of barbecue potatoe chips and an orange drink.

On my way back from the store, I gave Gary his items and I was about to give him his change, but he reached and took out the five-dollar bill and said keep the rest. I didn't think too much about it, so I went back upstairs to my room. Each time he saw me going to the store, he would stop and ask me to bring him something back, and tell me to keep the change. But on this particular day, he decided to talk a little bit more. He told me that he was trying to talk to me the other day when I was on the phone and I was ignoring him.

I apologized and I asked him, "Why do you keep giving me your change?" Then he told me he liked me and wanted to get to know me better. I wasn't ready to start a new relationship, so I smiled and kept walking. Gary wasn't giving up so easily. He asked me out every time he saw me, and each time I would tell him no. He kept asking me out until I finally gave in and said yes. We sat outside on the steps and talked about ourselves and what we wanted to accomplish in the future. As we began spending more and more time together, he asked me if I would be his girl. I told him yes. He started taking me out to eat and to the movies on the weekends.

One night we were sitting in the living room talking,

and I noticed that he was wearing the same beige shorts the guy had on in my dream. I said out loud, "It was you I had dreamed about." He was like, huh! Then I explained to him about the dream I had of a man wearing beige shorts. He made fun of it and said in a deep Barry White's voice, "You dreamed about me baby," and then we laughed.

Since our relationship had gotten more serious, I wanted him to meet the rest of my family. He met my mom and my step-dad previously on Rock Street. My mom liked him because he was tall, dark, and good looking, with jet-black wavy hair. However, my step-dad wasn't impressed by any of that. He was looking at our age differences. When I met Gary, he told me that he was "thirty-two" years old. (I later found out he was forty-two years old).

One night Gary and I were going out for dinner, and I told him to pick me up at my grandma's house. He called to let me know he was on his way. After I hung up the phone, I thought, Oh no, Grandma is in the living room. I was hoping I would run outside before she saw him or his truck. When I met Gary, he was self-employed and drove a big old bread truck, he sprayed painted white, and I thought for sure that he was going to pick me up in it and it was going to be the joke of the day.

Meanwhile, Grandma was sitting in the living room on the phone talking to one of her sisters. I crawled. Yes, I crawled on the floor towards my grandma and whispered to her, "Grandma, I have a friend coming over and he is older than I am. I want you to meet him, so please, don't say anything crazy," and then she laughed. About ten minutes later, Gary pulled up in front of the house.

People were going to the door, trying to see who he was and what he looked like. Then, I heard my grandma tell her sister she had to go and meet my friend. As soon as she hung up the phone, I ran straight to the back praying, "Please, God, don't let her say anything crazy."

Gary made his way onto the porch, and people were going in and out of the door to meet him. Then I eased my way towards the living room to hear what my grandma was going to say. She got up from her chair, went to the door, and looked Gary in the eyes, and said "hello," and turned towards me and started laughing. That was it. I was afraid she was going to start cracking jokes about his truck. On our way out, I noticed that he was driving a Buick. Thank God. Neither my grandma nor any of my other family members cracked any jokes that night about our age differences nor had the opportunity to crack jokes about his truck. However, they saved them for the next day.

Most of my family liked Gary from the first day they met him. On the other hand, my step-dad and my aunt, couldn't get passed our age differences. They tried everything they could to get me to stop dating him.

One day, my younger sister and I were sitting in the living room watching television. My aunt came home and out of the blue, started throwing hints at me. She started talking about a friend of hers, had a daughter who was dating and older man and he gave her worms. Can you imagine that? I thought what in the world is she talking about? My sister told me not to worry about it because she was just jealous. But I knew it was her strange way of showing her concern. Nevertheless, she later accepted our relationship.

Another occasion was, my step-dad came over and told me he had seen Gary downtown with his wife and three children. Which was a lie. Gary had been divorced and he had only one daughter. Then a few weeks after that, my step-dad tried to set me up on a date with a guy he'd met. I was over to my mom's house when this man came over and introduced himself while my step-dad was standing behind him listening. He told me he was interested in getting to know me and he gave me a watch. I thanked him and I went back to our apartment.

Later that day, Gary came over for a few minutes to talk and he saw the watch. He asked me where I'd got the watch from and the man was standing outside and I pointed towards him. I said that's the one who gave me the watch. (I was young) Then Gary got the watch and put it in his pocket and left. I thought he was going to throw it away or something.

That night, Gary came back and brought me another watch. I asked him what did he do with the watch that man had given me? He told me he gave it back to that guy and told him that I didn't need anything from him.

I tried to imagine the look that was on that man's face when Gary gave him back the watch and told him that. A few days later I saw the man standing outside and he called me over and confirmed what Gary did. He said, "Your boyfriend gave me back the watch and said that you didn't need anything from me." "Hum", I thought.

About six months later, my granddad passed, and from that time on, my grandma was never the same. I have seen other loved ones pass, but it never had an effect on her like the passing of my granddad. My Grandma had always been a strong woman and she didn't go around with her head down, and she never gave up on God. She kept reading her Bible and praying asking God to help her through her crises. When she was making his funeral arrangements, her sister, the landlord, was urgently requesting the rent money. The family thought that since she was family she should have let her slide for that month. But she didn't. And my grandma didn't argue about it, she paid her rent and left it alone.

About three months after that, everybody started moving out. My grandma and aunt had gotten an apartment together and later bought a house. My younger sister and I got an apartment together and my older sister and her husband got an apartment. A year had passed and I'd gotten pregnant with my second child. I told Gary that was pregnant and gosh, he did a 360 degree turn around.

He started saying he saw me in a car with some dude in front of our house. I was in shock and swearing at him in my mind. "Where is this coming from?" I thought. I had never been involved with any other man since I'd known him. I was not that type of girl, *I am the good girl.*

I was trying so hard to figure out what other man he was talking about. Gary went on about this invisible man for two weeks. Here's this guy, whom my whole family liked, and he was talking crazy. By the third week, Gary came over and apologized, saying, "I'm sorry, I'm sorry. I didn't mean it."

He had never given me any reason why he said that, and still, until this day, I don't know what prompted him to act that way. But, I knew one thing; I was going to get him back. I wanted to hurt his feelings just like he had done mine. I accepted his apology and I grudgingly waited for an opportunity to get back at him. I was still learning him, therefore I didn't know what strategy to use to make him upset. While I was waiting for an opportunity to plan my game, the baby was coming.

My sister Poot called the ambulance and Gary. Then she called Gwen. Gwen and her husband were the first ones to arrive at the hospital. After I arrived, Gwen went to the delivery room with me. She was so excited; she threw a rag over my face. Gary finally arrived and met Toisy in the hallway.

Five minutes later, my baby girl was born. She had a head full of jet-black wavy hair and she looked just like her daddy. Gary was so excited! He walked up and down the hall and suddenly, it hit him, he started wondering why he wasn't in the delivery room. Later that evening, he asked me why he wasn't in the delivery room. It was something that made him go, humm. However, he didn't realize that during the delivery I didn't want to change partners in midstream. Besides he got there when her head was out.

After being in the hospital for three days, it was time to name the baby and go home. My future stepdaughter Chelby, named her little sister Cheyenne. Gary and Gwen were there to pick us up from the hospital. Gwen grabbed the baby and started walking towards the door. Then Gary gently got the baby from her and walked proudly out the door. She made a face behind his back and we laughed as we walked down the hall. But, before we left the hospital, a man stopped us and gave Cheyenne her first dollar. From that moment on and everywhere we went with the baby, someone would stop us and tell us what a beautiful baby we had. Gary always held the baby because he got a kick out of people stopping him to see the baby because it made him feel like he was famous; he was truly a proud dad.

3

Married

After the baby and I had settled in, Gary moved in with us and boy that was a mistake. It was six people living in a one-bedroom apartment with six different personalities sharing space. It was like fireworks going off every minute. One minute, Gary and I would be arguing and the next minute, my sister and Gary would be arguing and then my sister and I would be arguing. Eventually, as time passed, the arguments settled down. Not only did things settle down at home, Gary's business slowed down as well. He decided to get a job delivering pastries. One day, he brought home a twelve-inch cake that served at least eight or more people. My sister, while everyone else was asleep, would go into the kitchen and eat just about the whole cake and leave two slices and a heap of crumbs.

The next evening, when Gary came home from work, he would go into the kitchen to get him a piece of cake, but he only found cake crumbs. He got so furious and he and my sister would start arguing and cracking jokes about each other. Gary walked into our room shaking his head, saying, "I can't believe she ate the whole cake." After a year had

passed, Gary and I decided to get our own apartment.

We found a two-bedroom apartment back on the West side. Once we had settled into our new apartment, I got a job as a cashier in the canteen at a local hospital. On my first day at work, I met three interesting women who all professed to be Christians. Although I wasn't saved or into any religions, I heard about God and Jesus when I was growing up from my Grandma, and at church on Easter' Sunday. However, there was more I had to learn.

The first lady I met was a true worshiper. She was a very nice and polite person with a good attitude; she reminded me of my mom. I could see Christ in her life, she actually demonstrated Christ-like characteristics. The second one was a hypocrite, one minute she would talk about God and the next minute she was on the back dock having an affair with the delivery man. I didn't know too much about being a Christian, but I knew that was wrong. And the third one was the youngest one amongst them. She was trying to teach me about Christ, but she had some real issues of her own to work out. One day she would be happy and talk to me about Jesus and the next day she wouldn't speak to me at all.

This went on for about a month. Her "Dr. Jekyll and Mr. Hyde" personality irritated me; therefore I had to pull her to the side and have a little talk with her. I waited until she was in a good mood to talk to her about her split personality. So one day she came into work smiling and saying, "What's up girl? God is good, ain't He?" As she proceeded to talk more about God, I kindly interrupted her and said, "If Christians act like you, I don't want to be one." "What," she asked. Then I said, "One minute you would talk to me about the Lord and the next minute you won't speak to me." 'Then I said, "You can either speak to me like you have good sense or don't speak to me at all." From that moment on, she began to have a better attitude towards me and we got along great.

Back at home, Gary and I were still adjusting to sharing space and learning more about each other. Gary and I got into a disagreement about him letting a female neighbor in our apartment when I wasn't home. He told me about her being over there, and I didn't think anything was going on between them, nor was I jealous of that woman by any means whatsoever. Trust me when I say that! However, I told him I didn't want another female in our home when I wasn't there, because first, he wouldn't like it if I had another man in the apartment when he wasn't there, (remember the watch incident) plus rumors could get started that way.

After I had finished explaining that to him, "honey," that man went over to that lady's apartment and got that woman and brought her back to our apartment and told her to tell me that there was nothing going on between them. I was in total shock and thinking this man has lost his mind. And the look that was on that woman's face was as if she was surprisingly flattered. Right then, I noticed, although Gary was much older than I was, (twenty-two years to be exact) he wasn't so bright. That woman would have never known about our conversation if he hadn't gone over to her apartment, got her and brought her back to our apartment and told her, to tell me there was nothing going on between them. From then on, every time I tried to talk to him about something, he would put me on the spot, and sometimes he made it looked like I was a jealous wife. Jealousy had nothing to do with it. Another reason was, there was a young lady in our unit, having an affair with a married man across the street from our apartment and everybody knew about it, except the wife. I was just keeping trouble like that from coming to our apartment.

The next day, on my way to work, I was still upset about what had happened the day before. I saw a co-worker on the bus. She knew that something was wrong with me, so I told her what I was upset about. After talking to her I felt a little better and it helped ease the tension that I had all balled-up inside. However, after we got to work, I put my things away and went to my register. A few minutes later, I noticed that people were coming to the front looking at me. And I thought to myself, 'why is everybody coming to the front looking at me," and **BOOM**! It hit me. The news had spread to the other employees and I had gotten mad all over again. I was thinking, "Why did she open her big mouth?" I felt so ashamed and embarrassed. However, from that incident I learned that if I didn't want my business out, I should talk to someone I could really trust or keep my big mouth shut. After my shift ended, I went home and told Gary what had happened; he just looked at me and went outside to work on the car as if it was no big deal. To me it was.

Gary started coming on my job two days a week to have lunch with me and on this particular day, he unknowingly sat at the table with the co-worker who told our business to the other employees. I went over and sat down. Everything was going great, just peachy, until, all of a sudden, out of nowhere; he got on the subject about how easily I get upset, which he was referring to the past argument about our neighbor. His mouth was like a river, and like a river, it was running. He started telling her how I got mad because he let someone in the house.

I was sitting there thinking he got some nerves. I composed myself as best as I knew how and calmly explained my side. While I was talking he interrupted me and said, "She's mad right now." I thought," Who is this man? Where did he come from?' When lunch was over, Gary left and I went back to my register anticipating the end of my shift.

Finally, it was 4:00 p.m., and time to go home. As I was leaving the job, I was thinking, "I can't wait to get home and let him have it." However, after taking two busses and two trains, by the time I got home, the anger had dissipated. Thank you Jesus! When I arrived home, I calmly walked into the door, went towards Gary and told him not to be on my job telling our business. Besides, that's the woman who went back and told the other co-workers what I told her. All he said was, "Oh, I didn't know." I thought....*Duh.* That was the end of our lunch dates and the beginning of the end of our communication. I called his mother to get some clarity about his mind set. After talking to his mother, she couldn't figure it out either. However, it helped me to get to know her a little better and I started calling her on my lunch breaks. Then I started visiting her at her house and helped her with whatever I could help her with. Sometimes she watched the kids for us and she showed me how to make a sweet potato pie. Then we started going over to her house for family gatherings.

And the Gospel Was Preached

Back on the job, a co-worker started to have the *"Do the right thing,"* talk with me. She was referring to Gary and I living in sin. ("Shacking up" was what grandma called it, and let the church folks say, Amen) I wasn't saved, so living in sin didn't bother me. However, she was not giving up on me, nor did she criticize me in any way or used any condemning words or compromised her belief to win me over to Christ. She kindly planted the Word of God and let God be God and do the increase.

Ok, Ok, I get it. It is time to get married. I began to think about it, and the more I thought about marriage, the more it seemed like the right thing to do. Besides, Grandma always talked about fornicators were going to hell. I went home hesitating about talking to Gary after I'd turned him down a couple of times. So when I got my nerves up and talked with him about getting married, he said, "I have been saying that all along," Then I researched and found out what we needed to do. After we got the information we needed, we took a blood test and found a judge, and got married.

Then it was time for us to tell our family. My mom was in the hospital having a Sickle Cell Anemia crisis. She didn't say too much because she was in a lot of pain, but I could tell in her eyes that she was pleased and my sisters and grandma were happy for us as well. Then it was his turn to tell his mom, but he made me tell her, and when I told her, she said with joy, "Well it's about time." Overall, both of our families were happy for us. I went back to work and told my co-workers and everyone was so happy for us and they gave me plenty of advice on keeping my good man. Yes, I knew I had a good man ,but not a perfect man.

Reflection of my Man

There I was married to the man of my dreams -literally-a dream come true. A man I loved everything about. His wavy hair, his dark skin, and thick hands. A family man that provided and was a hard worker. Oh how I loved that man. I loved his smile, his eyes, and his faith. His strength, his laugh, O how I loved that man. The way he walked and the way he talked, ahhh his pearly white teeth and the twinkle in his eyes.

4

Celibate

When Sex Leave the Marriage

On our wedding night, we had sex for the first time as a married couple, and it felt right. Our bed was no longer defiled, but purified. We were no longer fornicators. We were now living as our parents and grandparents lived, an honorable life before God. But, I never thought that after a few short months of being married, I would become celibate for the next thirteen years.

Here's how it started. Gary had always initiated sex. However, I was initiating it on this particular night. Gary was acting strange, so I asked him what was wrong and he said, "I can't." I said, "You can't?" "Can't what?" I never thought "I Can't." He looked embarrassed, so I asked him again what was wrong. I was thinking that he was feeling sick or something. He didn't want to talk about it so we went to sleep. I waited a couple of days to see what was wrong. Every time I asked him what the problem was, he would get irritated and walk away. After two weeks had gone by and still no answer, I began to think that he was seeing someone else. What else was I supposed to think with no explanation?

Now two months had passed, and I continued asking him what the problem was, but all he would say was he didn't want to talk about it. Then I got frustrated and told him out of anger I was going to find me someone else; trying to get him to confess if he was seeing someone else. He would only get mad and totally ignore me and acted like it was his problem and I had nothing to do with it.

Now I needed to get out of the house, so I went shopping. A guy came up to me and asked me for my number. I was upset about my husband shutting me out about his "I Can't "problem. So I blurted out, "Look, I'm married!" 'I think my husband is seeing someone else. If you still want my number, you can have it." After telling him I was married, he still wanted my number; so we exchanged numbers and we talked on the phone a couple of times before we decided to meet up. Since I didn't know anything about this man, I wasn't going to meet him alone. I asked my sister Gwen to go with me, and we met him in the parking lot of a flea market. My goal was to find some answers to what kind of sexual withdrawals men go through.

As he walked over to the car, I got out and sat on the hood while my sister stayed in the car. We shook hands and started talking about each other's day. Once I'd gotten comfortable into the conversation, I asked him if he heard of men having any kind of sexual problems. He said," No, he had never heard of any sexually problems."(I didn't realize at the time, I was asking a guy around my age.) Then he started talking more about his background. While he was talking, I looked up into the sky behind him and saw lightning flashing. For some reason, I knew it was God talking, but I didn't quite understand what He was saying, however, I knew lighting strikes. So I kindly ended the conversation and my sister and I left and I never spoke to that guy again. Hey I wasn't trying to get my candy apple fried for no one.

5

Fighting Temptation

Nevertheless, I began to walk in lust no matter how hard I tried to fight it. It was a mind thing trying to take control of my body. I started fantasizing about famous singers and actors. I thought that picturing myself with them was better than actually cheating with someone else.

I was living a life of celibacy; a life someone had forgotten to tell me about. I wasn't living in sin, so why was this happening to me. Is there really a problem or is there another woman? I never heard the women in our house talking about men having sexual problems. This was something I had never imagined.

Nevertheless, temptation was staring me in the face. I had to make the decision to stay faithful to my husband or to find me a new love. I started to think. Do you Gary, take thee Alecia, to be your lawfully wedded wife? To hold and cherish in sickness and in health, for richer or poorer, until death do you part? "Yes" But celibacy wasn't in there. So, where did it come from? Was I the only one who was dealing with this problem? And why hadn't I ever heard the women in my family talk about it?

Moving along, after our female neighbor moved out, a guy moved into her apartment. I'm the type of person who stays to oneself. Gary was more of the outgoing person. He liked getting to know people and trusted everybody. After Gary was getting along great with our new neighbor, our neighbor and I would talk from time to time. As the months went by, I enjoyed talking to our new neighbor until one day, unexpectedly; he told me he liked me. I promise, I never gave him any kind of signs or said anything to him that would make him think I was attracted to him in anyway, because I wasn't. He was around my husband's age and this was the first time I'd noticed that older guys were attracted to me. I guess some of them thought that since I was married to an older man, I liked older guys.

However, his comment shocked me. I knew I had to tell Gary, and "Oh Lord, why did I do that?" One night Gary and I were sitting in the living room talking about how our day went. Then I told him his *"friend",* our new neighbor, was trying to hit on me, but to not say anything to him about it. I was telling Gary that so that he could see that he could not trust everybody. Guess what? A few days later my neighbor and I were on the front porch talking about what he did in the service and out of the blue he said, "Your husband told me you said I was trying to hit on you." My mind went blank. I started mumbling under my breath, that blabber mouth.

Then I said to my neighbor, "I don't know why my husband would say that, he was probably trying to see if you liked me." He knew I was lying because he knew he had said that and he didn't look me in my face when he was saying it.

So I walked back into our apartment and waited on Gary to come home. When Gary came home, I met him at the door and said, "Gary, why did you tell that man what I said? He said, "What?" I said, "You told him I said he was flirting with me, and I told you that so you could be on the lookout." And as usual, he would act as if it wasn't a big deal. Gary wasn't the type of person who held grudges. He kept talking to our neighbor as if he never flirted with me. After getting over another embarrassing moment, I was the one feeling guilty. Well, my neighbor and I continued to speak to each other, but he never flirted with me ever again.

The final temptation was, there was another guy who lived in the same apartment complex whom everyone in my family knew. He was the type of person that would date every female in the family, if he could get away with it. He stayed in the apartment above my cousin, Jewel. One day, when I was leaving my cousin's apartment, he walked with me and asked if I had a boyfriend. I said, "No, you know I'm married." Then he said, "You need a boyfriend on the side just in case your marriage doesn't work out." Then I asked him, "What if I get caught and my husband put me out?" Then he said, "You can go live with one of your sisters." I said, "You crazy!" I may be twenty-three years old, but I'm not foolish. I later thought about what he said and tried to guess how many women have actually fallen for a joker like that and broken up their happy family for a two piece snack when they have steak at home. Later that week, he told me he had a picture of me in his apartment. I laughed and told him he was lying, because I knew I didn't give him a picture and neither did my husband. Besides, he had never been in our apartment. But to my surprise, he went into his apartment and came out smiling holding a picture of me when I was in middle school and it was the ugliest picture I had ever taken. I snatched the picture and ran. I didn't find anything humorous about that at all. I later found out he'd stolen my picture out of my cousin's photo album. Who in their right mind would steal a picture of a married woman? That was the most eerie feeling I had ever experienced. And every since he showed me my picture, I kept my distance from him.

6

And Saved

Since I was back in school, our money had gotten tighter and we had to make some adjustments. We lived in our apartment without gas for the summer, however, to get by, we used a portable electric stove to cook and to heat up bath water, or we would go over to my sister's house to take a shower. Gary's workload slacked up, and he was out of work for weeks at a time. Our money had gotten even tighter. My mom helped us out with whatever she could and a friend of hers helped Gary get a job doing demolition, but first he had to be certified. While Gary was going through training, our rent had gotten further behind and we had to move. Since my great-aunt owned the house I grew up in, we asked her if we could lease it. She let us rent it for two-hundred and fifty dollars a month. We moved out of our apartment before an eviction notice was given, and we were back in the house I grew up in.

But before we were settled in our new place, my grandma passed. We buried her in the country next to our granddad. A few weeks later, Gary was stationed back in Washington D.C. He was gone for days and the days turned into months. He would come home for two weeks out of a month.

Then he was stationed in St. Augustine, Florida. On that trip, he took the kids and me with him. It was a long, eight hour drive. On our way down, we stopped at a restaurant that had the best "all you can eat" breakfast bar in town, and we ate like hogs eating a hog, we had bacon, sausage, pork chops, eggs, and grits and enjoyed every bit of it.

It was night when we finally left Georgia and entered into Florida; we crossed a huge bridge that seemed like it was at sea level, and the water was so blue and beautiful and looked peaceful. However we quickly got across it.

Once we made it into St. Augustine, we checked into our hotel and went straight to bed. The next morning Gary went to work, and the kids and I went shopping and took a tour of the city. When Gary came home from work, we all went out for dinner. I couldn't believe I was still struggling with sexual desires on our beautiful trip. I didn't bother telling Gary about it because I knew he wouldn't talk about it. I hoped that it would go away, and it did for a little while, but it came back.

On our way back home to Georgia, Gary said we went down to Florida with a thousand dollars and came back with only two hundred dollars. Hey, that was our first time ever leaving Georgia; we had to enjoy ourselves. Gary wanted us to keep traveling with him on his trips to Florida, but I didn't want to mess up the kids' attendance, so the kids and I stayed home.

On the weekend when Gary was in town, we would sit in the living room talking and drinking wine coolers. He did not know that drinking and lusting weren't a good combination, and were adding more to my afflictions. Later that year, Gary was stationed back in Washington, D.C., but this time he was gone for four months and came home only one weekend a month. On the weekend he came home, I noticed that we had become distant from each other, kind of like strangers and we argued a lot.

When he came home, he acted as if I had done something to him. He came in and said a smart remark to get me upset; quit school and get a job. He complained to my sister Gwen that I needed to get a job, after he had bought him a truck. He talked about that truck as if it was his new love.

No matter what, I wasn't going to quit school, besides; I was tired of working in restaurants. Then he started joking and saying I had a boyfriend. I thought he was saying that to see if I had been fooling around with someone else while he was out of town. He was getting on my nerves, so I went to the Laundromat to wash our clothes. I met an old man there and we were generally talking. I told him that my husband was accusing me of having a boyfriend and I didn't understand why. Then the man told me to look in his wallet and he left.

Once I finished washing and drying our clothes, I went home and put our clothes away. I fed the kids and put them to bed. Gary was taking a bath and his jeans were in the chair in the living room. I was thinking should I or should I not? I should. "Oh Lord," I found a picture of a woman. I tried to act like I didn't know anything about it. So I waited until the next day when he accused me of having a boyfriend. And when he did, boy did I act a fool. I said, "Who's that woman on that picture in your wallet? 'That's why you keep saying that I have a boyfriend, and that's your sex problem right there." In shock he said, "That's my niece, that's my niece. She lives out of town." I thought about it for a minute, he could be right because I haven't met her. But for some reason, I didn't believe it.

The next day it was still on my mind, I wasn't saved but I started calling upon the Lord to show me the truth. I said, "Lord, if this is his niece let it leave my mind but if it's not, don't let it." And it didn't. The next day, I called his mother and told her about the picture that I found in Gary's wallet. I described the girl, and told her the name that was written on the back. Her description and the name on the back of the picture didn't match. After finding that out, I didn't believe anything else he said. I stopped believing that he loved me. Strife and resentment had built up. I found myself feeling betrayed and unloved. I was faithful to a man who was betraying me. I believe if you love someone, you wouldn't hurt them. I was tired of being married. I said out loud, "Oh Lord, why did I get married?" I couldn't trust him anymore nor could I live with him, so I asked him to leave. He left and went to his mom's house. After I calmed down, I was missing him like crazy, but he never knew that. After a few weeks had passed, he stopped by to check on the kids and me to make sure that we had everything we needed. I finished school and signed up with a temporary service. I had enough assignments to pay the bills.

After three months, he moved back in and I was so happy; we hugged each other all night long. He told me the truth about the girl in the picture. He said she was a waitress in a restaurant he and the guys ate at and she liked him. Then I asked him, "But why did you take her picture and put it in your wallet?" Then he said, "I was just stupid." I agreed. However, we tried to move on, but I couldn't get past trusting him so quickly. I decided not to put my heart in our relationship again, and when he told me that he loved me, I would roll my eyes up in my head, and I wouldn't say nothing at all. He kept saying, "I love you." Then I said, "What is love?" I don't believe in love while leaning over a hot stove and my elbows bouncing up and down because of the heat from the oven. Then the lie he told came back, and I got upset and I left. I drove over to my younger sister's house. Once I got there, she told me she was praying for me because she dreamed she saw me in a car accident. I thought about that for a moment because I was upset when I left the house and I was almost in a car accident. We talked for a while and then I went back home. It was late, so I went straight to bed.

The next evening, I was watching TBN Christian's station, and I saw Marilyn Hickey, a bible teacher, talking about being saved and how Christ gave His life so that we could have eternal life. All I had to do was say this confession, *Dear God, I confess that I'm a sinner and I believe that you sent your only begotten Son, Jesus, to die on the cross for me, I accept Him as my Lord and Savior and I ask him to come into my heart right now.* That is it. I was saved. All of a sudden, I wanted to stop cursing.

So I decided to stop using profanity on Sundays, and

eventually I stopped all together. The more I watched Marylyn Hickey, the more I was changing inwardly. However, everything didn't just change overnight; it was the beginning of a process. Gary was stationed back in town. He came home trying to aggravate me. He would come in, sit down and brag about all the things he bought for me. He knew I would get upset and start arguing with him. But before he got there, I prayed and asked God to help me not to argue with him. When Gary came in I was standing in front of the dresser waiting on him to say something smart. Then he started talking about all the things he bought for me and what a good man he was, hoping that I would get mad and start arguing. But I politely said, "Hello, how are you doing?" He looked surprised. Then he started bragging about the car he had bought me. And I didn't say a word and from that day on we acted like civilized folks. However, I was tired of depending on him and hearing him brag about the things he bought for me. I asked God to help me get my own stuff, and from that one prayer, God had showed up and showed out.

The car Gary bought me started having major mechanical problems and it eventually broke down. We didn't get it fixed because it cost more to fix it than the value of the car. Gary promised he would get me another one. But

I knew he couldn't because he had his car note to pay. I got aggravated with him and God. I didn't know God so well, I started smart mouthing Him. All God was trying to do was comfort me. I was walking down the street upset about riding the bus and God was trying to put his loving arms around me and speak words of encouragement.

But I told Him I didn't want to hear it and I wanted to be left alone. And Boy! That was a big mistake, and for a few short weeks, that's what God did. He left me alone. That was the first time I ever experienced God's presence leaving me. I didn't have any peace at all, no matter where I turned. During the Christmas holidays, we took another trip back to St. Augustine, Florida, and our hotel was on the beach. I couldn't enjoy the beautiful ocean; it was like a brick blocking my mind. I apologized to God asking him to forgive me. It was as if he didn't hear me at all. I kept praying and begging God to forgive me, and when He finally did, I never refused His comfort ever again.

Moving on from that unpleasant experience, I wanted to get a permanent job. Then I thought about what Marilyn Hickey said about tithing and faith. So, I put it to the test. I sent ten dollars to her ministry and the next day, I got a call from the temp service placing me on a three day work assignment. I kept tithing, and the more I tithed, the more assignments I got. Then I ended up with a permanent job with a large corporation making twelve dollars an hour working in the accounting department. After being on the job for three months, I was able to buy my first used car, it was a Chevy Cavalier. I could tell Gary was getting jealous because I wasn't depending on him as much. He said that I didn't have to work because he made enough money to take care of the bills. Yea right!

God wasn't through blessing me. I told Gary that I was going to start going to church. I wasn't actually going for real, it was just talk. However, Gary suggested that I should ask my Aunt Eunice if the kids and I could go to church with her. So I called her and asked her if the kids and I could go to church with her and she was so delighted to have us join her at church. The kids and I met her at her home and we went to church from there. However, when we got there, it wasn't like I had imagined. I thought, once I walked into the church, I would feel a gush of wind blowing through my hair and hear angelic music playing like I'd seen in a movie.

The kids and I joined the church at the altar call and were baptized three months later. Every Sunday, we would start our morning in Sunday school. I enjoyed going to Sunday school, because I could ask questions. Reverend Ausberry was the teacher. Mother Wallace was the assistant teacher. Deacon Vickerson was the superintendent. Each one would give us their understanding and experience about God. We were there for two years when I discovered that I could talk to God about anything. God had become not only my father, He was my friend. I was in church fantasizing being married to single men, but they never knew it nor did I give anyone signs of interest. It was a mind thing. I talked to God about the desires I was battling within and wanting to give in to temptations and I didn't want those feelings anymore. God is so awesome. He helped me too overcome those desires by applying scriptures when they arise. Then he wanted to move me to another church. Why? I had no earthly idea. I had a nagging in my spirit to leave the church, but I didn't know where to go. So I stayed at Mount Gilead until I was clear about where we should go.

One day, I was driving home from work, listening to a gospel station. I heard a man teaching eloquently in the Spirit on a chapter in the Bible. I said out loud, "Now that man knows what he's talking about." But I wasn't sure if he was local or out of town. Everyday I would listen to the radio trying to catch his broadcast.

I finally caught the church name. It was Word of Faith, and it was six miles from our house. The following Sunday, I decided to visit the church. Since this was my first time visiting another church, I invited my sister Gwen to go with me. It was on Mother's Day when we visited and immediately I felt different. After going for a few Sundays, and at the prompting of the Holy Spirit, we joined at the altar call.

I went home and told Gary about my experience and a couple of Sundays later he visited and joined. But, because of his bad knees he stopped going after three Sundays. While I was there, I learned about the gifts of the Spirit, Spirit discernment, and the foundation of Christianity. After growing to a new level in Christ and learning what my gift was, God moved me back to Mount Gilead and I became the assistant teacher. I was so excited about what I had learned and how I had grown spiritually, I was a leader in two ministries. Some members would stop in and tell me what a great job I was doing. One of my mentors had gotten a little envious, but it didn't destroy our friendship.

Now everything I'd learned at Word of Faith was tested on the job. For instance, I met a woman who was unhappy with her life and envied the life she thought that I had.

She wanted a house, a husband, and kids. Having all of that wasn't smooth sailing; it was work. And she didn't know about the celibate life I was living. (Some people think the grass is greener on the other side). I put to use what I had learned while working as a cashier, which was to keep my mouth shut if I didn't want my business out.

This girl told all of her business to the other co-workers and she thought I acted like I was better than them. It's funny how a person tries to read your life and be wrong, she was on the outside looking in and got a different picture. One mistake I made was talking about how good my husband was and his buying me nice things. If I had known that would have put jealousy in that woman's heart, I would have never mentioned it. She started throwing hints at me; talking in a general conversation with the other co-workers, about people who keep their business to themselves are usually being beat on by their husband. Good Lord, a mind is a terrible thing to waste. That woman's envy grew until she formed a click against me. They started doing all kinds of crazy things. One lady even missed a day of work just to follow me home to see where I lived. The other one was trying to use witchcraft on me. Whatever she tried to put on me, landed on her; a rash spread over her body. Even though they thought that I didn't know what they were doing, I learned how to smile at my enemies and let God be God and fight my battle. As His Word says, "No weapon formed against me shall prosper..." If I didn't experience what I had, I wouldn't believe that scripture today. However, in the end, we all got along. One even came back and confessed to me that she knew that God was with me. Ha.

There was another situation that taught me to obey God when He tells me to leave certain people alone. This particular person turned out to be a Judas. This lady and I ate lunch and took our breaks together. God showed me a dark cloud around this lady in a dream, and he told me to stop hanging around her, but I thought it was a bad dream. Then, He told me again through a mutual friend that this lady was nothing but trouble. Yet, I had to find out the hard way. When we were on our break, she tried to get me to bad mouth certain people on the job, so she could go back and tell them what I said. I told her I knew what she was doing, but she denied she was doing anything. Another thing that gave her away was, one of the women she tried to get me to bad mouth had answered a question I asked my friends on our break. I told my lunch buddy, it was all right and I distanced myself from her.

She really hurt my feelings because I thought that she was a good friend, and I hadn't done anything to her to make her turn face. I held a grudge against her for a long time, but I had to let it go and once I let it go, she got fired.

Then I met another young lady whom I thought would be a true friend. This lady knew the Bible and could quote any scriptures and tell me what chapters they were in the Bible. I went home telling my husband about my new friend that I could talk Bible talk with and she wasn't about all that foolishness. (How many of you know that the devil knows the Bible, too?) With her, I opened up a little more about my goals and a little bit about my family, but not about my life of celibacy. We talked about the crazy things my husband and I did to embarrass the kids.

I told her about the time my husband and I went outside and shook our groove thang in front of the kids while their friends were over. And how the kids ran to tell us to go back in the house, and my husband would crack lame jokes and he would be the only one laughing at them.

However, she too wanted all of that. When God told me to leave her alone, it didn't take but a second for me to do that. I was trying to figure out how I was going to tell her because I didn't want to hurt her feelings and build strife between us. But the only way I knew how to tell her was to be frank. So the next time I saw her, I told her point blank. "I don't know what it is about you, but God told me to leave you alone." Maybe that didn't come out like I wanted it to, but I wasn't going to be hard headed like I was the last time.

I didn't know what happened to her, but she started acting weird. Each time I took my break, I saw her and she would act as if she didn't see me. When I was going up the escalator, she would be going down and when I was going down she would be going up. Or I would be walking East and she would be walking West and vice versa. This happened every time I took my break. All I was thinking was Lord, I don't know what's wrong with this chick but she done flipped out.

After work, I went home and told my husband what she had done. He told me the lady saw me, she wanted me to think she didn't. So I started sending her motivational poems to ease the tension between us and she sent me some hell destined scriptures. And that was the end of that. I'm glad I heeded to God's voice about her and what I learned from that experience was that God tells us to leave certain people alone for a reason. It's not always necessary for a bad reason and sometimes it is. God sees the heart of every man and woman's motives. Just move on and if you are hurting, know that God can heal you.

7

When Loved Ones Leave

As the years went by, the kids had grown and were in middle school and doing great. Our marriage had gotten better, and things around us were changing. Every year or so, someone went home to be with the Lord. If it wasn't someone in Gary's family, it was someone in mine. It was in 1997, when Gary's older sister passed. She was the first sibling I met. Then two years after that, his mom passed, he took it pretty hard. After her funeral, Gary became ill and deeply depressed. He went to the hospital and was diagnosed and treated for pneumonia.

He stayed in the hospital for three days before he was released and he worked in town a month before traveling back out of town. His depression had gotten worse and he became isolated. I did everything I could to help comfort him and suggested that he should talk to someone about his feelings, but he refused any outside help.

I called one of his sisters and told her how he was feeling and I asked her if she could talk to him. She called and talked to him for a while and listened to him express his feelings about their mom passing. From then on she called to check on him, and as a result, their relationship grew closer.

He was so excited to have gotten closer to his sibling. Later that week, my great-aunt passed-the mean one- but, no matter how mean she was, I didn't want to see her gone. I remember a couple of years before she passed; I was learning how to walk in love. My mom was talking to her on the phone and I asked to speak to her just to say hello. I got the phone and said, "Hay Auntie." She said, "Lisa, this you? I said, "Yea." She said, "Oh go to hell."

My feelings were hurt so badly, I said, "That is it. 'She better never ask me to do anything for her ever again." Everybody was making excuses for her, saying she had always been like that, don't pay her any mind. But I didn't want to hear that. My mind was made up. Then a few weeks after that, I was laying down watching TV. She called and asked me to bring her two wings and a biscuit. I politely reminded her that she told me to go to hell a few days ago, and she called the wrong person. She needed to call one of my sisters and I politely said goodbye. Then I called my younger sister and told her that her Aunt (I was being sarcastic) wanted two wings and a biscuit and I told her I wasn't going to get it. Then I hung up the phone and laid-back down, but something inside of me wouldn't let me rest. I knew it was God nagging at my spirit. I said, "Lord! I've been nothing but nice to her and I have taken all that I'm going to take from her. I'm not taking her anything!"

However, God proved me wrong. I couldn't rest until I went and did what she asked me to do. So I got up fussing all the way to KFC, to get her three wings and a biscuit. After I got her three wings and biscuit and took it to her, she was sitting on her bed looking sad. She thanked me for bringing her food and she ate it like she hadn't eaten in days. And she was a little nicer to me every since that day.

For her funeral service, I did her home going program and I picked the song, "When it's all over here, I'm going home," And from that day until now, I have been the chosen one to do our family home going programs. (It is not always easy being nice to someone who is constantly mean to you, but God used my aunt to help me to understand love never fails)

In 2000, my cousin Wayne went home to be with the Lord. Wayne was the first person I tried to rebuke the devil out of when I first got saved. One day I was over his house, he was acting hyper. I said, "Come here." I put some oil on my hand and I said, "Come out of him you unclean spirit." He looked at me and said, "What are you doing?" I laughed and told him that I was rebuking the devil out of him. He said," Oh," and walked up the street with his friend. I can recall the day of his passing, God told me to go over to his house. I didn't go because I was tired from running around all day. So I made plans to go over the next day, however, later that evening we got a phone call saying that he was in the hospital. That is one experience that has left me with the question, what if? And I learned that, I may not always understand why God tells me to go places at times that seem inconvenient to me, but it's important to obey His voice.

Two years later, Gary's sibling whom he became close to passed. I was afraid he would get depressed and isolate himself like he did when his mom passed. But to my surprise, he didn't. He grieved for a couple of days and decided to focus on the good times they shared. Gary got sick again, he was diagnosed with congestive heart failure. He was in the hospital for two weeks and released with all kinds of medications.

We were sitting in the living room when his supervisor called to check on him. He told his supervisor about his illness and when he was going back to work. Since he was a foreman, he didn't think his job would cause him any harm to his health. When he went back to work, he worked for a month and the company downsized. He was the first one to go. A friend of his who worked there told him they let him go because of his health condition, but they didn't want him to know that.

So he decided to start his own business again by doing small demolition projects. He got a contract with an associate. He didn't know too much about bidding for those types of jobs, so he underbid himself. And he didn't make any profit for himself, because most of the money was going towards the materials and employees' salaries. He tried to get more clients, but it just didn't work out for him. So he got a job with another construction company. However, that job only lasted three months because he had gotten sick again and because of his health, he had to resign. His health had gotten worst. But this time he was diagnosed with diabetes and kidney problems, and other illnesses he never told me about.

He was so disappointed because he wasn't able to provide for his family liked he used too. At one point, he thought that material things made me happy, for the kids, it did, because it was their nature. I told him that I enjoyed him spoiling me, but I wasn't a materialistic person. I wanted to help him get his mind off of his problem, so I took him out to dinner. He barely touched his food because I was paying for it. A man and his pride, I thought. I told him not to worry about it, besides he wasn't like some of those gold digging men who want a woman to take care of them. I must admit, it was hard but God saw us through.

The Breaking of a Man's Pride

After he accepted the fact that things had changed, I went and got my first pedicure. It felt so good. I wanted Gary to get him one. Boy did he refuse to go along with that. He said, "Pedicures were for girls, and his doctor clips his toe nails." And he didn't budge. Again, I said, "A man and his pride."

One day he decided to go and sit with me while I got a pedicure. When he walked into the shop, he saw a man in a chair getting a pedicure. He was so happy he got into a chair and got him one. And that was his first of many pedicures. Then he started reminding me to go and get our biweekly pedicures.

God had given us a financial blessing, Gary was so proud he could do some of the things he used to do for his family, and help other people as well. A few months after, God told me to resign from my job. I thought that He was joking. I had plans to excel in the company. Besides, our finances were back on track. People were going to think I'm crazy if I resign and Gary wasn't going to go for that. (People are not going to understand why God tells us to do certain things, and to be honest, but it will manifest).

I continued to go to work as if God didn't say a word. Then all of a sudden, my right knee started making a popping sound every time I walked. I went in, prayed and asked God to confirm that it was Him who told me to resign by healing my knee. A few hours later the popping stopped. I thought about how I was going to tell Gary that I was going to resign. So I went back to God in prayer and said, "Lord I need you to confirm to Gary this is your will for me to resign." After I prayed, I went to Gary and told him it had been on my heart to resign. After talking to him, and getting his support, I told my boss and co-workers that I was leaving the company. They were surprised to hear of me resigning and on my last day at work they took me out to lunch and wished me the best.

Then I had to face some of my critics. My mom was the first one and then my sisters. But I knew that it was God's will, and what God says, goes.

Since my plan to advance in the company was out of the question, God had plans for me to advance in his work. So I relaxed for two weeks while I was waiting on God to give me directions. For the next four years, my life had become busier than ever. I homeschooled my daughter for a year, became the PTSA President, I did workshops and training, shared turns taking my mom to dialysis, planned birthday parties, Mother's Day and Father's Day lunches, family gatherings and home Bible study, most of it at no charge. (Don't worry for my work was not in vain is somewhere in the Bible.)

Every year, my sisters and I gave our mom a birthday party. I would sit back and watch how much it meant to her. She was so happy to see her children and siblings, coming together, bringing her big bags of gifts. However, there was one year we didn't have her party because everyone's finances were a little tight. I knew my mom was expecting a party because she asked me what we had planned near the time of her birthday. I didn't want a year to go by without doing something for her birthday.

So a month after her birthday, I took her to get her first pedicure and she enjoyed it very much. And when I took her back home, she bragged to her boyfriend about how pretty her feet looked. I was so happy, I was able to do something for her she never had done before.

Five months later, her health turned for the worst. After I had picked her up from dialysis, she was complaining about pain in her right leg. I took her home and two hours later, she called and wanted to go to the hospital. Then I went back to her house, picked her up, and took her to the Sickle Cells Crisis Center at the hospital.

I waited a few minutes to see if they were going to admit her or give her pain medication and then release her. She was sitting in the chair rubbing her leg saying, "I'll call you when I'm ready." For some reason I couldn't move. It was like I had frozen as I stood behind her watching her rub her leg. Then she slightly turned her head looking over her left shoulder and she said again, 'I'll call you to pick me up. Then I left and went home. About three hours later, the hospital called my sister Gwen and told her we needed to come down to the hospital. By the time we got there, our mom was unconscious. The doctor told us she had three strokes. While he was talking, someone from an organ donor organization called, asking us if we would like to donate any of her organs. My mind went blank. I felt like my spirit had left my body and another one stepped in and took control.

Then another doctor came into the room and told us she was on life support and dialysis. Right then I knew my mom wasn't coming home. Gwen and I didn't see any reason why she should continue on life support because none of her other organs were functioning. But my younger sister, Poot, didn't want to take her off life support. She cried out, "Seven days, give her seven days. 'That is God's number of completion." We waited until we talked to our brother before we made any decision. After talking with our Tony, he agreed with Poot, and we waited seven days before we agreed to take her off the machine. I knew that it would be the longest seven days of my life.

We met at the hospital for six days and on the seven day, we all agreed to take her off life support. The Priest came in and we gathered around her bed and prayed, then left the room. Afterwards, the doctor came in and removed the life support and the dialysis machines. Once all the machines were gone, we went back into her room and stayed for twenty minutes talking about the good times we had and went home.

Our uncle John helped us with her funeral arrangements. We decided to bury her in the country next to our Grandma and granddad. Two days after her funeral we went over to clean out her apartment and her locker at work.

That evening, I was walking around the house thinking about my mom and thanking God for seeing us through another difficult time. I noticed Gary was in the living room watching me. I asked him, "Why are you watching me?" He said, "It hasn't hit you yet!" He was speaking of the grieving process people go through after losing a loved one. I told him God was keeping me strong and I will miss her and I will cry sometimes, but I know that she is in a better place. I guess he thought I would go into a depression like he did when his mom passed. He kept his eyes on me to make sure I was all right.

Over the past five years, Gary and I had gotten closer than we had ever been. We became something we never were before, we had become better friends. We went just about everywhere together and talked and made fun of how some people acted.

One night, a storm came through the city and knocked the power out. We sent the kids over my sister's house. Gary and I sat in the living room by candle light and watched a movie on the lap top. He wanted to open up to me about his past experiences with people he dated, who didn't appreciate him. He talked about one girl in particular from his high school who liked him. For some reason he just wanted me to know, and I just listened and didn't say a word.

The next day we were out in the yard planting flowers and he continued talking about this girl from high school. For a moment, I thought he was going to tell me he was having an affair with her or something. Then I said to him, if she is on your mind so much, let her cook your dinners and take care of you, then, I had to go back to the picture I found in his wallet years ago. (You know how we do.) Then there was a brief moment of silence as I watched him wondering what was going on with me. But to my surprise, he wanted to see if I would get jealous. Since he wanted to play, I decided to play with him.

So I waited a couple of days later to plan my game. One morning I got up early and went to the mall for a couple of hours, and then over to my sister, Poot's house. I was gone for three hours before Gary called around looking for me. When he called my sister's house, I was in the car on my way home. He asked her where I'd been, but she didn't know because I didn't tell anyone where I was going. I told her to tell him I am on my way home. When I got home, he was waiting at the door with a smile on his face and he asked me if everything was ok. I told him "Yeah, everything is peachy." He had dinner ready, we sat down and ate. Afterwards, I thanked him for making dinner and kissed him on his cheek. A few hours later my sister called me to make sure I was at home. I told her yeah, and asked her why? She told me that Gary blasted her out because he thought that I was on a date that she had set up. She told me word by word what he said and we laughed about the whole thing.

After we hung up the phone, I told Gary he didn't have to worry about me cheating on him; if I wanted to cheat I would have done it a long time ago. And no matter how crazy I acted, he was still the one for me. Then he told me no matter how crazy he acted, I was still the one for him.

Then Gary told me he felt like he was a burden to me. Because he saw woman at the hospital pushing her husband in a wheelchair and she was wearing shades to hide her frustrations.

I told him, "Yes, it gets hard sometimes and that's why I go out to have time alone. Things are different and it's not easy, but I am going to stick it out." I was going to trick him and tell him that I was pregnant, but after hearing how he felt, that would have been a bit too much. But I told him I thought about telling him I was pregnant so I could see his reactions. Then he said with his eyes all bucked, rolling from left to right, "Girl, don't play with me like that." Then I started laughing.

One night Gary's gout flared up, I took him to the pharmacy to get his prescription. On our way home he took his pills, but he had to wait a few hours before they took effect. By the time we got home, he couldn't get out of the car because he was temporarily paralyzed. He told me to go into the house and he would be in later. I wasn't going to leave him outside alone, so I went into the house and got us a blanket, and we slept in the car. That really did put a smile on his face. He saw how much I loved him, and he didn't have to guess how I felt about him based on someone else's feeling towards their husband.

However, that didn't stop him from showing his overly protective emotions for me. I was outside talking to a neighbor he wasn't particularly fond of. He sent the kids outside, one–by-one to tell me to come in the house. I guess I wasn't moving fast enough, so he started flashing the outside flood lights. I couldn't do anything but laugh. It took me three months to convince Gary to be kind to our neighbor. He eventually did and they became good neighbors.

But, I knew his illness and impotency was part of his insecurities. No matter how many times I tried to tell him it's ok, it was a part of him that was never content. And the other part of his insecurity was a guy who was supposed to have been his friend, knew my husband was impotent, called my husband and bragged about all the young women he was dating (but they only stuck around for a week).

One night his friend called our house while he was on a date with two women who were obviously intoxicated. He put one of the ladies on the phone talking flirtatiously with my husband. Just like I wasn't moving fast enough to come in the house when he sent for me, he didn't end the call fast enough. The only thing I did was looked back and Gary gave me the phone. I told that woman to put her friend back on the phone. When he got on the phone, I told him not to call our house with that mess; you got that."

He said, "Ah, yeah." From that moment on and even until this day, that man hasn't spoken to me and I never lost a wink of sleep over it. The next day, my husband told me that his friend calls him saying things indirectly to make him feel bad or try to make him jealous, and the reason why people don't come over was because we lived in the ghetto. "I told my husband his friend was jealous of him, and look at how many times he had been married, and all the young women he tries to get. What we have is genuine and we have been brought together by God himself, and it's ordained. He just wanted a fine young woman like you have, but he just can't get one. And God blessed us with a home and we weren't in the ghetto, it was ghetto people living in our neighborhood."

Now after twelve years of marriage, Gary decided to talk about his impotency. He told me he tried and it didn't work, and he wanted to start taking some pills that were out on the market for guys who suffer SD (Sexual Dysfunction). Since he was on so many medications, I told him "I was content without having sex after all of these years and don't worry about it, I made it this far without sex, and I can do without it." He just smiled. (Then I tested him to see if he would actually say I can have sex with someone else. Not that I was going to do it, but to see if he would actually say it.) I told him I do have desires and they are strong

60

sometimes. He said, "It's ok, but I'm not going to say that you can sleep with someone else," and then we laughed.

After talking to him I learned for years he was feeling hurt, scared, and frustrated with himself and afraid that I was going to leave him because of his impotency. I told him if I wanted to leave him, I would have left a long time ago. And I told him, no matter what he is feeling, he could talk to me about anything. Then I told him about the dream I had. I dreamed that I had another baby and he just listened. Then he explained to me that the baby was me and it represented the beginning of a ministry. I was thinking God was going to heal him of his impotency or do to me as he did to Mary, Jesus' mother. Let the Holy Spirit overshadow me and I conceive a child. Yes I know that's funny now, but that is exactly what I was thinking. Looking back now, my husband knew exactly what the dream was about. He never said anything too much about it, but he knew. God was revealing more about me to him, than he was to me. We didn't discuss it too much because we were making plans to get our pedicure.

8

"When It Rains It Pours"

It was the anniversary month of my mom passing, and a tornado came through the city and knocked down two huge trees from a yard of an abandoned house. The trees damaged part of our roof and crushed our SUV like pancakes. The impact caused the ceiling in my son's room and hallway to fall. My son was still in his bed sleeping and covered in sheet rock when Gary ran in and woke him up. We were thankful that no one got hurt. Unfortunately, there were two dogs under the car hiding from the storm. One dog was badly injured and the other one didn't make it. We didn't know who the dogs belonged to, because neither one of them had on an ID tag.

I called a few animal hospitals to see if we could get help for the injured dog. I found a veterinarian that said he knew of a woman that would sponsor the dog's medical treatments, so we took the dog to the vet hospital and explained to the veterinarian what happened to the dog. The veterinarian was so furious about the dog's injuries; he wanted to give our insurance company a piece of his mind for not having the trees removed sooner than they had. He assured us the dog would be taken care of and we left. The veterinarian called us that evening and said he wanted to call the news station so they could do a report on the dog, because he thought that it was an injustice to the dogs that our insurance company didn't act quick enough to have the trees removed. Later that night a news reporter called and got the story.

Next, we had to find a contractor to repair the damage to the house. We drove around and found a contractor a block from our house. Gary went over and talked to the contractor and told him we were looking for a contractor to do some repairs on our house, and if he could come by and give us a quote. A few hours later he came by to look at the damages and gave us a quote for the labor, because we were buying the materials ourselves. We signed the contract and he said that he would start the following day.

Since that was taken care of, my sisters and I had a girl's night out. We went to the mall and took pictures and went to Piccadilly for dinner while we waited on the pictures to be developed. I called home to check on Gary to see if he was ok. He was laying down when I called and he told me to have fun.

Gwen and I made plans to go to the movies

afterwards, but Poot wasn't up for going, when the pictures were ready, we sat in the food court and divided them. We started talking about the good old days and laughed about the crazy things we used to do. We started with Poot, because she was the craziest one in the family. We talked about how she got into a fight with a boy and tried to make him wash his hair in dirt. And how two of the boarders had gotten so mad at her for picking at them; they were actually going to fight her. Then we talked about when Gwen would come home and tell Grandma about some spirit she'd seen. Poot and I thought that she was making that up because she came in the house late and didn't want to get a whipping. And then it was me, Lisa. I was the one that stayed in the house most of the time, *"the good girl."* I'm not saying I didn't do any mischievous things; I just never got caught doing them. For instance, if someone put their open drink in the refrigerator, I would go in and take a sip, because I knew someone else would get blamed for it. But my cousin, Jewel, put a stop to folks drinking her drinks.

One day she made a tobacco drink and put it in the refrigerator. I went in the kitchen and saw the cold drink and I grabbed it thinking I was about to quench my thirst. I held my head back and let it rip. It was the most awful thing I had ever tasted. It was filled with hot sauce and tobacco juice. I quickly put the drink back and closed the door and walked out of the kitchen like nothing happen. The next day, Gwen threw up from something she ate and she was the suspect for drinking the tobacco drink, while I stood back laughing, knowing that it was me who drank the drink.

And Grandma always told us not to run in the house. One day I was running through the kitchen and a glass fell off the cabinet and broke. I ran out the room before anyone came in and saw me. My grandma came into the kitchen and saw the broken glass. I was walking behind her saying, "What was that?" She said, "This glass must have fallen off the cabinet." Then I picked up the glass and walked back out the room as if I didn't know anything about it. O let us not forget about the time when Grandma told us to come in the house when the street lights came on. One night we decided to come in ten minutes after the lights came on. When we walked in the house grandma was standing behind the door with a belt. Something told me that she would be behind the door with a belt so I sent Gwen in first. And when she went in, a belt went across her but while Poot and I ran passed her laughing. However, back then Gwen didn't see anything funny about that.

After my sisters and I talked and laughed for a while, we hugged each other and went home. On my way home,

God was talking to my spirit. I can remember saying out loud, "Wait, I'm almost there." I called home to make sure everything was ok. My son picked up the phone. I asked him was Gary all right He said," He is lying down but he hasn't drunk his orange juice." I told him "I was on the highway and I'll be home in a few minutes."

Three minutes later I entered the house and went straight to the bedroom. I asked Gary if he was ok and I heard him say "Yep." I turned on the light and got on the bed. Kneeling towards him looking in his face and asked him again; while I was asking him if he was ok, he took his last breath. I got on the phone and called 911 and told the operator my husband stopped breathing. She coached me to give him CPR and told me "help was on the way, continue to administer CPR until they arrive."

The firemen were the first ones to get there. Once they got there, one of the fireman started administering CPR and he asked me to leave the room. I went into the hallway and waited to see if they could revive him again. I heard one of them in there cracking jokes about our age differences. I couldn't believe what I was hearing, while in shock and in disbelief.

Then I called my sisters and step-daughter, and told them that Gary stopped breathing. Then the ambulance team arrived and, they tried to revive him on the way to the hospital. My Uncle John and Aunt Sadie came over and stayed with the kids.

Both of our families were at the hospital when the doctors came in and pronounced him deceased. Then we left and went home. My sister Gwen came over and got the children, she wanted me to go with her. But what I wanted was to be alone and think about what had just happened. After my sister and the kids left, I went into my bedroom, and fell on the floor and let out an uncontrollable loud wail.

I sat there crying and praying asking God to help me. I had to pull myself together for the kids and I still had to make his funeral arrangements. My sister Gwen was worried that people were going to take advantage of me while I was grieving. God told her not to worry, "*He got this*," and no one was going to take advantage of me. I had such a great peace and confidence like a lion because God was with me.

The contractor and his crew came over the following day to do the repairs on the house. I told him to "repair the roof only, because my husband passed last night, and I will call him back to finish the rest." Then I paid him in full for the roof.

When he got on the roof, he started showing me all kinds of problems. I told him don't worry about it just do what he was paid to do and nothing more. He continued showing me all kinds of problems and he was getting on my nerves. Once he finished, he brought me another invoice. That was it. I told him to "get his stuff and everybody with him and get out of here." His cord wrapped up so fast it sounded like it was singing.

The next day I started making my husband's funeral arrangements and someone else was actually judging me. They thought that since they didn't see me crying and hysterical, I didn't have any remorse for my husband.(Lord have mercy) He even tried to put me in my place, but I showed him how to make a quick U- turn. He didn't know me like that, besides I just met him a year before.

On the day of his funeral, our families gathered in a circle and prayed. After the repast, we got into the family car and I was talking to God and said aloud, "That wasn't bad, God is seeing me through this." I learned that God wants his people to learn how to let go and have a peace of mind when He calls a loved one home.

My Struggle

After the kids and I got home, there was a note on the door from the animal advocacy. I didn't think much of it because I was trying to process that I just buried my husband and our house was still in a mess. Two days later, a lady from the animal care advocacy came to our house inquiring about the injured dog. She told me that a veterinarian called her company and said that "We left the dog under the car too long, and he contacted the news people." Then she showed me a copy of the news report. It stated that we were the ones who abandoned the injured dog. I told her none of that was true and the dog wasn't ours. We were the ones who took him to the vet. We didn't know anything about any animal rescue unit, and we didn't have twenty thousand dollars to remove those trees. We had to wait on the insurance company adjuster to approve the removal. We later found out the veterinarian had lied to get free publicity for his veterinary hospital.

The next morning, I got a phone call from a woman asking to speak to my husband. I told her he was deceased and I could tell in her voice she was shocked and she never knew my husband. My husband's *friend,* who did the late night calling, had put her up to call my house and ask to speak to Gary. I knew it was him, because I changed my number the day after my husband passed and he was the only one who had my new number because he wanted to help with the funeral service.

Oh, that is not all now I am getting to the good part. An old friend of mine came by to see how the kids and I were doing. I told him we were doing fine but I needed to finish the repairs on the house. He quickly asked, "You got the money from the insurance company." I paused for a moment because I didn't want to say anything I would regret later, and the flesh didn't have any problem taking over. So I politely said, "Gary had some health issues he never shared with me, and the insurance company came across it in his medical records, therefore the policy was annulled and they only paid out what we put in it. I paid for my husband funeral services myself."

The nerves of some people, I couldn't believe that joker was in my face talking about insurance money. Don't get me wrong, I could talk about my business to family, but that joker wasn't kinfolk.

Oh Lord, how much more could I take? My cousin Jewel came over to make sure we were ok. I told her that we were fine but I still needed to finish the work on the house. So she got the family together to finish the ceilings and remodel the bathroom. I did worry about the crushed SUV because I was planning on selling it to the junk yard. Too late, someone came and stole it, the lawnmower and weed eater.

Ok, I'm still hanging in there. It's a month after my husband's funeral and I needed to start making money so I could take care of the kids and pay the bills. Before my husband passed, I joined a small church about five blocks from our house. I met a guy there who was an excellent businessman and he was going to help me promote my business. Everything was in place and I was well on my way. So I thought. I went back to church hoping to continue with his help, but to my surprise, out of nowhere, for no reason at all, he did a three hundred and sixty degree turn around; he was talking about and I quote "the Bible states knowing someone is to sleep with them." I didn't know why he was saying that but I wasn't a harlot and that big bad wolf wasn't going to catch my little red riding hood on any day. I didn't know where his mind was or what he had in mind, but he made it clear that I wasn't going to receive any help from him. And he made sure that I was no longer welcomed at that church.

I told God, "*THAT IS IT.*" I will keep in touch with You, but I am not going to church anymore. After that I didn't want to have anything to do with church, period.

A month later my step daughter invited us to her home in Florida. I was afraid of driving a long distance because Gary did all the driving when we went out of town. I tried to think up every excuse not to drive out of town. But God told me to go. After I wrestled with God for two days, as usual, I lost. I called and told her we would leave Friday night and get there sometime Saturday morning.

My son wanted to stay over his new friend's house, while my daughter and I went and visit Chelby. Instead of leaving Friday night, we left Thursday night. On our way down, the highway was filled with huge tractor trailer trucks and each one moved to the side out of our way as we drove for six hours. Then I knew it was God who told us to go and He was with us. After we arrived, the next day she treated us to the Disney Theme park, we had so much fun, we stayed three days and returned home.

When we got back to Georgia, I called my son Zay, and told him we were on the way home. Since it was late, he wanted to spend the night over to his friend's house. I thought that it was fine and he needed to be around guys his age right now, so I told him he could stay over.

The next day, he came home, ate and left out heading back over to his friend's house. He was doing this everyday for a week. He was spending more time over to his friend's house than at his house. The he started having trouble in school and got kicked out and he stopped going to church. I tried talking to him to see what was bothering him, but he wouldn't open up to me. At first I thought it was an outlet for him to deal with my husband passing and it would pass, but it didn't. It went on for days and I didn't know what to do. By this time my physical strength was gone and I couldn't take anymore, I said, 'Lord, I give up. I sat back for a couple of days trying to figure out what to do. I decided to look into who his friends were and where they lived.

When my son came home to change his clothes and left again, I followed him. After I found out what house he was staying in, I went in and talked to his friends' mother. I asked her, "Why are you letting my child stay over your house so long?" I found out her son was doing the same thing and she said, "She'd rather for her child and his friends to be safe at her house than in the streets getting into trouble." As a mother of a rebellious child, I understood that clearly.

But I had to do something to get my child back home and on track. So I decided to home school my son and invited his friends who dropped out or got kicked out of school and tutor the ones who were still in school. I provided snacks and sometimes I took them out to lunch.

After spending time and getting to know each of them, I learned that they were not bad kids; they just needed some guidance and to know that God loves and cares about them, and to value their education and never give up on their education. Before the study group ended, two of them went back to school and each one gave their life to Christ.

If God would have told me ahead of time he wanted me to go and reach out to a gang, I would have never done it. The word gang would have scared me. He used my son's rebellion to get me to go into an area I would have never gone on my own, and because of my son's rebellious attitude, five souls were saved.

"If It Aint One Thing, It's Another." Ray Parker Jr., must have been singing that song based on his life experiences. When that trial was over, there came another one. I was in the kitchen cooking dinner when my daughter, Diamond, (is what she calls herself) came home beating on the door with blood running down her face. I saw the blood and wanted to know who did it and where they were. She told me that a boy on the school bus was showing off in front of his friends and pushed her. I Yelled, "Where is he?" She pointed at the bus as it was passing the house. I ran outside and told the bus driver to Stop that bus, Stop that bus!

The bus driver told me she was taking the boy back to the school. The kids and I jumped into the car and headed straight to the school. When we got to the school, I was so upset. I was walking up and down the hall looking for him. Since I didn't know what he looked like, I ended up passing him in the hall. The assistant principal took Diamond into his office and cleaned off the blood. I wanted to talk to him and hear what he had to say about hitting my daughter. But the principal wouldn't let me let me talk to him without his parents, so I asked him to call his parents. The boy's mom had scheduled to meet with me the next day.

Before we arrived at the school, the principal investigated what had happened on the school bus. He said, "All the students on the bus stated the boy started the whole thing." His mother was so disappointed and hurt to find out her child had done such a thing. He apologized and was afraid because Diamond told him that she was going to get her cousins to beat him up. I assured him no one was going to beat him up and I asked him not to put his hands on her or any girl again. A couple of days later I asked Diamond how things were going with the boy at school? She told me he wanted to be her friend and carry her books for her and they became friends before the school semester ended.

9

I Just Wanted to Get Out

After the passing of my husband and dealing with life's trials and tribulations, I just wanted to go out and meet new people; but not date. I was in a thrift store looking around to see what they had, when a man came over and introduced himself. He started talking about some items in the store and nervously asked me for my phone number. I gave him my number and two days later he called. We talked on the phone for two weeks before we met up and went to the mall. He told me he enjoyed my company and wanted to take me to the movies the following weekend. So the following weekend, we met at the movie theater, he bought the tickets, and we went in to enjoy the movie. About twenty minutes later his cell phone rang. He went out into the hallway to answer the call and came back in. He told me that it was his sister who called him. And for the next thirty minutes, he walked in and out of the movies pretending that someone was calling him. He would come back in and sit next to me and stare, hoping I'd ask him who is that who keeps calling him. It wasn't my business therefore I didn't ask.

After the movies, we walked to the food court and he bought us dinner and we talked about our likes and dislikes, but nothing about starting a relationship. After we finished, we got up and headed out the door. He grabbed my hand and I kindly pulled it away because I was thinking that we were just hanging out and not on a date.

After we left the mall, we went our separate ways. About twenty-minutes after I got home, he called me and told me what a wonderful time he had. I told him I had a good time as well. Then he told me to ask him, how he felt about me. I told him I knew how he felt because I had seen it in his eyes. Then he kept asking me to ask him how he felt. And I kept telling him I already knew. Then he said, "You mean to tell me, it's not important to you to know how I feel about you." Then I politely said, "No." He went on and on blabbing about me not wanting to know how he felt about me.

After he finished blabbing, I said, "I really had a good time tonight, and I don't know how we went from laughing to this. I didn't mean to upset you in any way, I just wanted to get out of the house, and have a good night." My sisters and I had a good laugh off that one, and if he would have asked me for his ten dollars back for the movies, I would have given him twenty dollars. Then there was another young man I met who was having trouble with his aunt. At times, he would stop by the house and tell me about the problems he was having with his aunt. I was trying to be a good soldier by listening and offering advice. I encouraged him to go to church. He found a church down the street and he would come by and talk about his new walk with the Lord.

Then one night, around nine o' clock, this guy come over to my house just to talk. I told him he is going to talk through the burglar bars because I didn't open my doors at night. His whole facial expression changed. I guess what I was saying to him was contradicting what he was thinking. But I knew one thing; he wasn't getting in my house.

Finally, a secret admirer came forth. My husband had told me for years this particular man liked me. But I didn't believe it because I had great respect for this man and he taught me about the Bible. This is how I found out he had a crush on me. After Gary passed, he too would call and check on me and the kids, to see if we were alright.

Each time he called, he would mention something that was going on in my neighborhood. Like the remodeling of the school up the street, or the apartments that were being renovated down the street. It didn't dawn on me until my sisters and I were talking about him. At first it was funny, but after a while, it wasn't so funny.

I never confronted him about it because I didn't want to hear him confess to liking me. I keep in touch with him, but not like I have before. I told a mutual friend of ours about his secret crush and she couldn't believe it. Yet, I could tell it was sweet gossips to her ears. She said "He knew of everybody else's business, but he never told his." I wasn't telling her about it to start any gossips about him. She is one person I could talk to without it getting back to him or anyone else.

After she had a good laugh, she said, "If I wanted to date him, it was alright. I told her he was way too old for me." Then she said I would be surprised what an old man is able to do. She was talking from her own experience with the older man she had married. But I told her no, I'll date a guy up to age fifty-five. And when I'm older, I'll move the age range up. But that age? No.No.No. Gwen told me that he probably thought that God told him that I would be his girlfriend or next wife. Then I told her that would be the first time I ever heard that someone said that God tells lies. LOL

Now it had been a year since the passing of my husband and God was telling me it's time for us to move, after ten years of living in our home. But before we move, I wanted to have one more family gathering at the house. The kids loved when our family got together and Gary loved how the women got together and fixed the food, while the men sat up the tables. He was the grill master, wearing his straw hat and looking good.

I started wondering if I would break down, when my eyes would see for the first time that my mother and my husband wouldn't be there. When the day came, it was just like always. The women prepared the food while the men set up the tables. We reflected on our loved ones who went home to be with the Lord. They are gone, but not forgotten.

When the day ended and everyone went home, I relaxed and thought about what a great time we had. There is nothing like family, especially my family. I know sometimes we bump heads, but I wouldn't change having them as my family for nothing in the world. When I was going through some of the roughest times in my life, they were there. When I needed something and if they had it, that gave it. And I thank God for them.

Moving On

We finally moved into a house that I have always wanted. It had more space than I could imagine. It was a split level house; Cheyenne and I were upstairs and Zay was down stairs, it was like he had his own apartment. Then God wanted to bless me with another car, a Mercedes. It was the car my husband always wanted.

Well, here comes more of life's trials and tribulations. My kids are teenagers now and we disagree about everything. They think they know everything. When it wasn't this one, it was that one. The arguing was stressing me out, I decided to let it go and let them run their course, because they have to learn for themselves. I have raised my kids the best way I knew how and no matter how good I tried to raise them, there were other people influencing them.

No matter how many times I have told them do not do this and don't do that, or leave that person alone, they still had to find out for themselves. I couldn't stop my kids from making their own mistakes. They have to live and learn for themselves. Life is a good teacher. I ask God to keep them in his hands and protect them. I also know the apple doesn't fall far from the tree, but I can surly say my kids did things I'd never done, and been places I had never been in my thirty something years. Nevertheless, I still love them and all the kids I have come to know through them.

I went to God for help and he showed me that my kids are teenagers and the times are different from the time when I was growing up. And the only way to deal with them was to love them unconditionally and talk to them at the right time and they will eventually come around. I thank God for His help. I have seen tremendous improvement with my kids. They are still growing and learning.

A while back I had lost my faith and stopped going to church. I was riding down the street and I saw a sign that said, "God will restore your faith." And now He has. It is good to be back in church again. My plans are to keep moving no matter what. I may have to stop and rest sometimes but I must, I must, I must keep moving, until the victory is won.

Final Thought

My husband and I were not perfect people, but we were perfect for each other. We were each other's helpmate, suitable for one another. I know there were times I was aggravated with the things he did or said and at times, he was aggravated with the things I did or said. I can truly say if there was hell in either of us, we both aggravated the hell out of each other.

Every marriage has its seasons of challenges. However, marriage is not about being in control. We both found ourselves at different times in our marriage trying to control one another. However, what I learned is that to move forward successfully, you must be quick to forgive, pray for each other, and esteem one another over than one self. Once God worked out my personal issues, I could love my husband better and vise versa. Each step was a mystery unfolded, but we made it through fifteen wonderful years... We both moved beyond the fears, pain to the healing process and had a successful marriage and you can to.

Scriptures for Reading

Abiding in Christ John 15:5
"I am the vine, you are the branches. He who abides in Me, and I
in him, bears much fruit; for without Me you can do nothing.

Anger James 1:19
So then my beloved brethren, let everyone man be swift to hear,
slow to speak, slow to wrath...

Divine Comfort John 14:1
"Let not your heart be troubled; you believe in God, believe in Me.

Forgiveness Mat 6:14
"Forgive if you forgive men their trespasses, your heavenly Father
will also forgive you. "But if you do not forgive me their
trespasses, neither will your Father forgive your trespasses.

Strength in Weakness 2 Cor. 12:9
"My grace is sufficient of you, for My strength is made perfect in
weakness.

Sexless Marriages

Sexless marriages are more common than one may think. Statistics show that 40 million couples in the United States are living in a sexless marriage   However, sexless marriages doesn't mean absent of sex, experts says its couples having sex less than 10 times a year. Some couples go on for years with not sex at all. Not only can this be frustration but also shameful, depressing, and prone for divorce.

Why do so many people find themselves in a sexless marriage?

There are many reasons why a marriage becomes sexless; age is not a factor or the lack of love. The two basic causes that can reduce sexual intimacy are physical and psychological. However, many people suffer from some health illness such as diabetes, cancer, or sickle cell disease. Furthermore, some medication may interfere with one's sex drive. On the other hand, dealing with internal and external sources such as body image, past hurt or dissatisfaction with sex can have a toll on one sex drive. However, with unresolved, it will causes a lot of tension, anger and even divorce.

The Big Challenges Sexless Couples Faces!

Sex is designed to strengthen the bond between couples and reduces the temptation of having outside relationship. However, if a spouse is continuously begin rejected he or she may become emotionally divided and seek to have an affair to fulfill a temporary desire.

Rekindling Intimacy back into the Marriage.

No one gets married to live in a sexless relationship, however, unexpected things happens to people beyond their control such as a physical or psychological condition. Furthermore, this may cause a spouse to live in confusing, resentment, or shame. However, there are many options couples can do to rekindle the intimacy back into their marriage. First, communicate. Communication is the first and most important step couples can take to get a clear understanding of what each other are feeling. In addition, it shows that you are concern about their feelings. Next, seek counseling. Many couples are ashamed and do not want people to know about the dilemma they are facing. Getting professional help is perfectly ok. Thirdly, talk to other couples who are coping in a sexless marriage and see what some of the things they are doing to keep the fire in their marriage.

Keep in mind. Not all marriages rekindle their sex life. Mines never did, I survived twelve years of no sex. I never thought that I would be living in a sexless marriage. However, my husband and I had the best relationship anyone could imagine. Moreover, we too had to deal the emotional rollercoaster and the temptation of looking for a new love. Now I conducts seminars on sexless marriage in hope of helping others sexless couples make the best of their marriage.

Gary and Alecia (Lisa) Hill

Alecia, and her sisters Gwen, and Poot in the middle.

Zay the Mac Man

Diamond doing her gangster lean

Can you guess who this is?

Hint.

He was in a dream I had.
You will hear more about him in my next book.

I hope you enjoyed this book and that it brought you laughter and understanding about things some couples go through in their marriage.

MAY GOD BLESS YOU

www.ingramcontent.com/pod-product-compliance
Lightning Source LLC
Chambersburg PA
CBHW071819020426
42331CB00007B/1540